The First Symphony

Don't Blame Not The Pen for Writing

Nadia Abu Shama

Dr. M.E. Fayad

@2024 AEEH PRESS INC

Brilliant Stars in the Sky of Literature and Writing

My sophisticated erudite student, Nadia Abu Shama, is of Algerian origin. She is a distinguished writer, an eloquent first-class person, and a talented writer. In a fantasy world other than that one you live, you are under a spell with her charming words, dancing with her messages. She is able to stir up all the sorrows confined in your deep recesses, so as to perceive the universe with the eyes of purity, serenity, and childish ecstasy.

She was born and brought up in the Babur Mountains - the city hanging at the foot of a large mountain with a geographical and historical heritage and home to revolutionaries during the French occupation, where great revolutions and battles took place. This region of enchanting and rare beauty was very isolated and remote from the capital city , just like a pearl or an expensive diamond concealed from all the world's eyes.

Collaborating with Dr. Fayyad, she has written thoughts, in the form of letters, and more than forty books, "Universal Symphonies." Examples of her masterpieces are: "The Novel of Al-Taffar" , "The Nude Body," "The Legend," "Dancing on Water," "The Ram Dancer," "The Gazelle of Al-Bawadi," "The Prisoner of the Past," and "The Rape of a Woman."

0000000

Dr. Muhammad Fayyad, an American of Egyptian origin, spent more than forty years, dedicating his life to the niche of knowledge, and spending the best days of his life in fruitful scientific research. Then generations, graduated under his supervision and sponsorship, believed in the value of science and learning, which contributed indirectly to the renaissance and development of America and other countries of the world through multiple expeditionary trips to spread knowledge around the globe.

Dr. Muhammad Fayyad contributed positively and globally to raising the status of human civilization in the world and participated in composing the "Cosmic Symphonies". Among his scientific, literary and reform works, he published ten scientific and permanent books and more than 500 scientific articles in the most famous scientific journals and conferences. And add to this, his striving to spread his innovations in the "Engineering of Unified Concepts", "the Unified and Stable Linguistic Engineering", "the Engineering of the Unified Field", and "the Art of Abstraction" . This is all with God's help.

Dedication

To that wonderful shooting star that deviated from the track of my soul and vanished far away. She left me burning earnestly with longing and suffering from the distance between us. Wherever go, I feel that I am separated from my other self, and that my soul is about to vanish in the thin air. I feel that I am heading towards the eternal kingdom of lunacy which is inhabited by all the lovers like me.

Nadia Abu Shama

Life is nothing but a moment, too short

If you are to live it in love, so smart.

Otherwise, is nothing but mere illusion

If you waste your days in idle delusion.

By: Abdul Aziz Jewaida

Dr. M.E. Fayad

Table Of Contents

1

How patient you are, my sweetheart, and open-minded!

How patient you are and tender-hearted!

When love distance seems too short

Through your everlasting beats of heart!

When with your heart, you wage a new war against

Those who are narrow-minded and extremist.

When with it, you make a call for love and peace

Among all the nations, the world countries, and all the human races.

You make it a peace banner on which is read:

"It is only love that triumphs over violence, death, bullets and blood.

It is only love that makes peace among souls, prevail and last.

It is only love that produces souls which are pure and chaste.

It is only love that implants the smile into our deep recesses before it draws it on our lips.

It is only love that brings happiness into the world and makes it spaces of roses of all kinds and colors."

How great you are! O great man!

Indeed, you were able to change many of the concepts adopted by humanity.

You are still striving to lead them to the greatest ways of comfort, tranquility, progress and human uplifting based on knowledge and complex mathematical theories.

You were also able to turn me into a princess, spreading and sharing her poems, in all universal languages, with all the world.

You made a real poetess of me with all standards of creativity.

You were the only one to interpret my poems, in all different languages, for all the world to see.

Sure, they will take great pleasure in my words.

However, they will envy you for my own heart where you dwell as though you were in a palace of the Islamic Granada.

They will also be jealous of you as you were uplifted, through the wings of my love, to the highest heavens.

Explain to them all my feelings, all my poems, all my words, and all my thoughts so that they know that North Africans have hearts that beat with love and set free white doves of peace, bearing olive twigs and green oak trees.

For sure, North Africans have hearts that never know the language of bullets, blood or what causes death, nor do they know the meaning of intolerance, racial or color discrimination, either.

2

Are you also suffering just like me?

My love, what are we supposed to call all these groans that haunt us from time to time?

Are you also suffering like me, and let your longing knives cut within you and tear you apart?

Perhaps, before now, you have never experienced love that drives you away from space and time.

You have never experienced the sweet taste of love and longing, that slaughters you from head to toe.

Never ever have you experienced the feeling of pain with pleasure with every strong heartbeat.

3

How long......?

How long will words and letters keep our reunion together?

How long will my messages keep tempting you?

And how far will they take you away from here?

How long will our hearts remain chained in the highest heaven, waiting for her liberation and release from the bondage of distance while we are waiting for our reunion?

How long will your bedroom remain gloomy with an empty bed over there?

However, all the bouquets of roses you intended to gift me remain stacked in vases, nourishing on water.

How long will your room remain gloomy in pale colors?

I stay away from you, away from your breath, and away from smelling the scent of your sweet body.

4

My Darling!

Darling! Would you take me to places you adored and used to go, but you were alone there?

Will you make of me an exceptional woman when you buy me a lot of jewelry and various outfits and make of me a princess excelling all the ones residing the palaces.

Will you dress my body in elegant wedding dresses, studded with glittering diamonds, and transparent fabric?

Will you race me like children on the edge of fields, and on the lovely beaches of the sea?

We will run together and hug each other as you lift me up and spin me around.

I love you as much as that exceeds the number of grains of sand on the beaches.

Your love is intricately mixed in my heart just like the most complex chemical equations.

5

Will you ever get bored of my letters?

Will you ever get bored of the letters of my language?

Or will you ever long for me and resort to the language of silence?

Or is it that the more I long for you, the more you long for me, and for all my writings?

Here I am back again to writing as before, or more than before.

So, I have readers and followers now.

Among them are those who would know how to dive deep in my letters to get what I mean.

Never ever say to me: "stop writing", and never ever ask me to stop loving you, as "writing and loving you" are the only equation in forming my entire life and my sentiments.

Now, I will confess to you all my heart prostrations in your love temple.

I will yearn for knowing all the minute details about you.

I will be craving you, just like the dry earth craving rain.

6

My love is so abundant

The first moment I longed for you, I forgot everything that had ever happened to me because of your silence and your arrogant mind.

I break down as soon as I come across your soul and read any of your letters.

What on earth is that which threw my love in your way?

What in the world is that which distinguished you from all humanity?

What kind of prayers did your mother use to say so that you obtained this overwhelming love that would sweep away everything in its path?

What kind of prayers, exclusive to your mother and special for you, which beg heavens grant you these flowing feelings.

 As a result, nothing is seen in this world but your glowing face, and no other outlet is known but that which leads to your deep feelings?

What kind of prayers that you have made as your protective and permanent arms against the drought in your life, and the end of pleasure in the procession of your life?

What great woman is your mother who gave birth to you, and made of you this wonderful, humble, merciful and tender human being, whose feelings are flowing and whose giving is plentiful?

What type of mother is this who brings me back to you whenever I feel offended from you, and whenever I decide to stay away from you.

So, she takes my hand and leads my heart towards you.

What type of mother is this who loved me so much without ever seeing or knowing me.

Yet, her soul is always flying with our love wherever we are. How good her soul is, while watching us everywhere!

What type of mother is this who, even after her death, wants us to be happy and for you to be the happiest man in the world.

She never asked us to pray for her, read the Qur'an to bring God's mercy for her, nor give away alms for her.

Rather, all she cared about you was not to be sad, nor to let the wound ever dwell in your heart.

She wanted me, by all means, to be by your side and close to you.

She wanted me to offer you all her previous services which she quitted offering you.

So, she wanted me to continue playing her role with you, without getting upset or bored.

She wanted me to always smile at you as she was used to.

7

The Quarters of your Charming Love

I know for sure that I will fall apart in every pace of distance.

I will do the impossible to have my abode built in you, and to have the walls of the place built within your noble being.

I will earnestly yearn for the life, I wished to live, in the quarters of your magical love, my darling.

8

God willing

I suffered pain much and more, as I have never tasted deadly bitterness and loneliness like this before.

However, every cloud has a silver lining.

After every dark night, a new bright morning comes...and God willing, I hope you will be my forthcoming sunrise, my happiness, and my love.

And everything that is beautiful in this world.

O you who implanted roses and purity deep in my heart whose birth you witnessed on your blessed hands...

And you made me love this life more than before.

9

New lifestyle

I will have to choose a new lifestyle, that is strolling down the lanes of my city, down the streets of the capital.

I will travel everywhere away from you so that I will never be alone with you.

I will reveal my madness when I tell about my passion.

I will embrace alone all the places where I go.

I will sit alone on the seashore.

I will have my food at a table with only one chair.

I will choose to go the distant roads to kill time waiting for nothing.

So, I will walk the long roads to get away from such places of communication.

Away from the virtual cities where we met and where I used to go.

I will cut off all the barbed wires to cross in search of you.

I will no longer be just like a message in your inbox.

I will no longer be like a world that you created once and excelled in.

I will put an end to that lovely kingdom with all its images, methods, library... and everything there.

I will become a very primitive woman and return to the bosom of nature.

I will return to my cities that are made of paper.

I will let our dreams' kite fly in the sky.

I will make paper boats to play with, on the surface of the stream, close to the running waterwheel.

No longer can I bear this crazy world where I have always felt your breath and known well the time when you would sleep and wake up.

I will abandon such virtual cities and palaces.

No longer can I bear the suffering of my heart.

No longer can I bear your being away from me.

I will learn how to be patient in my paper cities.

I will do away with all communication devices and phones.

I will quit all the world of communications that you created around me.

I will return to the time of Abdel Halim Hafez[1] and to the time of Gibran Khalil Gibran[2].

I will return to the world of Newton[3] and Edison[4] .

I will return to the true art of all the fine artists in Paris.

---

[1] a traditional sentimental singer[1]

[2] a romantic poet [2]

[3] an English mathematician, physicist, astronomer, alchemist....[3]

[4] an American inventor and businessman[4]

I want to go back, in the past, to the time of Alan Turing[5], Marie Curie[6] and Niels Bohr[7].

I want to sit at the table of Naguib Mahfouz[8], from which his creative revolution took place.

Now, no longer can I stand your being away from me,

As your love has overwhelmed all my organs,

And no part of my body was left without being reached.

[5]- English mathematician, computer scientist[5]

[6]- a Polish and naturalized-French physicist and chemist [6]

[7]- a Danish physicist[7]

- Egyptian modern novelist[8]

10

If only...oh! ..if .. only...!!

If only the distances were bound in my palms, and the winds were blowing between my arms!!

And if only you were the master of light, day and night, I would conspire with time, and run fast towards your heart, seeking your madness and your bed.

I would also awaken you from the slumber of fatigue and would invite you only to see the sunrise of this dawn with me.

The sun of which resembles us, as its warmth comes from us.

11

Describe to me the details of the pain

Did I have to suffer the pain when I loved you?

Or when I moved my fingertips over the eyelashes of your longings, creeping towards my sanctuary like a desert whirlwind that would stir up the sand of the dunes to conceal all the terrain there?

This pain has changed the map of my geographic place, so I was lost as if I were in a distant wasteland.

Every day I approach you, I feel secure, but every step away from you leads me to an endless maze.

Longings for you are drifting towards me, just like a professional mass army attacking an agent who violated the laws of the state and deviated from its system.

What kind of domination did you use to recite, like poems, on my ears?

Or pour on my heart like showers of rain?

Until I felt that I was perishing forever, or that I was an obedient prisoner who yielded to the laws of your whim.

I no longer found myself in your kingdom that you built on the brink of my heart and within the recesses of my soul.

All that happened was without my permission.

So, I last could find, within you, my abode and settler.

I don't know which of us crossed the line, you or me?

Who of us crossed the human terrain and began to follow the way of their longings yet shackled by their threads.

I was within you, just like a cocoon trying to escape from its silky fabric, and from the threads that it had woven with unparalleled miracle and genius.

Every time I suffered pain, I was trying to draw a painting, write a poem or prose, or give a loud cry, but I couldn't.

I used to run away from you seeking your eyes in order to paddle my boat in their sea using your eyelashes, so that I could sleep in them like a tear frozen due to long waiting and longing.

For sure, all these things, previously mentioned, have their pain: your closeness to me is pain, your distance from is pain, my longing for you is pain, and all that is about you and me is pain.

However, the pen has refused to write about this pain, or even take you to its journey of letters.

It has refused to make you dwell on the pages of books.

It used to suddenly murder people especially the loved ones with ink like bullets.

It prepared the best farewell for them.

It drew the slogan of both victory and defeat for them.

It would hysterically laugh to the point of madness, sadly cry and groan in pain, and joyfully dance in great ecstasy.

All the drops of its ink were used, like in a carnival, to write very carefully.

Then a cluster of words surrounded it like a jasmine collar.

However, when it endeavored to stand face to face describing you, it refrained, stumbled over and fell on the paper.

Then, I felt my pain grow more and more within me to the point that it took me to a place where I denied myself.

After that I didn't realize who I am, and where I am.

And when am I supposed to be here?

I returned from your kingdom with unknown identity and address.

I was lost and vagrant in your decorated cities that you built with your stubbornness and pride.

Such cities that filled the world with the children's joy, and with the teenagers' laughter and hustle.

At that time, you slumbered on my palm like a butterfly, in brilliant colors, celebrating the beauty of spring.

How much do I aspire to talk to you about morning and the dawn breathing in it.

About the first strands of light, about the flowering gardens, about the rainbow colors, and about the musical instruments.

Nevertheless, everything within me compels me to silence, and makes me roll at the slope down to your deep precipice.

You let me hear the sad lyrics of love; you let me hear the sound of the flute.

Following the astonishing map to your heart, I forgot everything that I had loved before I knew you.

I forgot my playing, freedom, and independence.

I forgot all the stacked books that I specially collected to read in the stages of my love and passion for you.

I forgot all the poems that I specially brought to recite to you.

At the time, it seemed to me that I would do more and more, and I would be so and so, but I could neither do, nor be anything but a wandering lover.

I did not realize that I would be the only person who would roam the kingdom of your depths and sit on the throne of pain and suffering in your presence and your absence alike.

So, I did not achieve anything out of myself.

I was neither a brilliant painter, nor a famous poet, nor a genius scientist.

All my dreams and aspirations were shortened by the laws of your femininity.

They made me a lover eager to meet, and eager to leave alike.

I became full of contradictions that shook everything within me: I want you, yet I do not want you at the same time.

I regard pain and love as synonyms that suddenly surprise and kill you against your will.

All your methods of fight will be futile to escape from the love claws of a woman of your strength, rebellion, and ingratitude.

I could only be an unrecognized victim in the court of your passion, because I could not untie my chains from your eyes and their sweeping sea.

You are like a flood, sweeping everything in your way.

I used to like perishing for you little by little, because I felt that I was growing mature with my eagerness for you.

With the sighs of your burning love, I obtain immortality.

I thought that you would record me in the history of mankind and declare that I surpassed Romeo in my love.

In the court of your soul, I was the only hero who was destined to be the guard to count your heartbeats and witness the dance of joys in your sky.

How eccentric I am to dedicate all my life under the mercy of a stubborn female who never looks back!

She mastered the language of clouds to sleep on them with her eyelids close.

She made various flavors of her love, which was colored and decorated with marks of hot desires.

Do not demand me to write about love, wound or pain, because I no longer knew how to read or write.

In your presence my silence has become my only language, and patience has become my only custom.

12

Sleep conqueror and creativity

I could not sleep, not because I was far from you, but I was accustomed to this lack of sleep since my childhood.

I slept fewer hours than usual, and I hated to wake up while everyone was asleep.

I used to keep walking up and down, from one place to another, and so this bad habit grew within me.

 And so, they called me the "sleep conqueror ".

Very often, they must leave the lights on when I sleep, so as not to turn them on when I wake up.

I remember the toughest punishment I had experienced because of my lack of sleep.

Once, I was sleeping with my ex-husband in one bed, then I woke up, an hour or less than an hour after sleeping, and then I got up to go to another place.

He tried to stop me from that and force me to sleep, and not to move.

After that I imagined that all my bones had melted from remaining motionless, and that worms would inevitably come out of them.

Then, I began to devise various tricks, until I got a license from him to sleep alone in another room.

It was the harshest punishment I have ever received in my life after all the punishments he had imposed on me.

And this made me hate sleep more.

In one of his discourses, the late Dr. Ibrahim al-Faqi[9] advised us not to sleep too much and to wake up early in the morning, because a day would come, when we would pass away, and we would sleep long without waking up.

This made me happy and I thanked God for that.

And I said: "There is one of the human beings who loves a little sleep."

So, I loved him after that, and I loved all his books and lectures.

As a matter of fact, whoever stays with me gets disturbed by my waking up.

Today, this bad habit is affecting my work, my health, and the system of my whole life.

I did not sleep …

I did not sleep, not because I adored you to the point of intoxication, but because this bad habit lives within me.

This anxious, sad state that I had experienced was evident on me.

Not only things from the past stuck to me, of which I was afraid, but also things I am afraid of its being inside me right now.

Twenty years later, I knew it was the strange moments of creativity within me.

They are the difficult birth moments of creativity in a certain field.

When words are to be born, this strange labor comes to me, and it continues to torment me until the words come out of me sequentially or scattered, important or trivial.

---

[9] Ibrahim Al-Faqi (August 5, 1950 – February 10, 2012) was an Egyptian human development and neuro-linguistic programming expert.

Most importantly, they come out like a fetus leaving the womb of his mother in labor. It is impossible for words to come down from me.

However, when they are born, a new strong start is born with them. How hard it is to be a talented creator!

It always torments you and makes you anxious, especially if you remain on the sidelines of life, not trying the field of creativity, and if you do not choose a path for yourself.

When you are far from the arena of creativity, you die, little by little, with every labor that comes to you, especially in the disunited Arab countries in which creative people die.

The groans kill them. They are torn one by one outside the circle of attention.

Labor will always live.

This creative person is the one who differs from ordinary people in many ways.

He is the one who has excessive sensitivity, in addition to permanent pains.

He is the one who lives in loneliness that tears one's eyelids, tears one's depths, kills one's being. So, no one is able to understand or support them.

Every creative person has strange rituals that make their state fluctuating between absolute madness and enlightened wisdom.

This is separated by one single moment.

This moment is just like the hair of a young child.

For sure, there is no escape from this state without what is generated by this enlightened mind.

I do not know if you experience such situations at the peak of your creativity and innovation, or if it is a case exclusive to poets, writers and artists.

You cannot write a single word until labor ends and birth begins. It does not matter whether this birth is normal or cesarean.

The most important thing is that these words pour like continuous sheets of rain.

So, bear with me in such cases of mine, because every father endures the labors of his child's mother, and has to live moments of fear and terror more than the mother herself until the fetus emerges, from between her legs, as a hot, soft piece of flesh with another life.

So, joy will overwhelm the mother, and spiritual feelings will envelop the father.

If fate were not to grant me the feeling of a child's labor, nor a father's fear and care, I would, for more than half of my life, live in labor alone.

For no one shares feeling.

Then I find myself searching for a father who will adopt my words and my innovations.

I try to find a name and a sponsor for them, but they remain orphans without a father. I keep searching all the faces for a face identical to the face of my word, or for a blood group with an extended artery to feed my creative works, like the umbilical cord that connects the fetus to its mother.

Before now, I used to wake up hours before dawn, but now I can only sleep at dawn. No soporific would avail me, nor did the will that I possess.

Do you think that your hypnotic embrace would be the only cure for me to sleep and rest?

Was your great tenderness and great interest in me what would make me fall asleep in your arms, or on your lap, like a little girl who would keep searching for the core of her lost tenderness?

You will definitely contain me, my beloved, and contain everything in me, change me and change countless things in me.

Will sleep, with your being with me, find the way to my withered eyelids, on which a dark tan appeared?

Will you stand as a barrier between me and what is bothering me?

Will you make me go to sleep effortlessly every night?

Is it in your ability to contain me and contain everything within me?

Surely you will tell me many amazing stories, while your fingertips touching my black gypsy hair.

Groans kill me when I am far away from you, and so do they when I am close to you.

I feel, when you are far from me, like a bird lost and away from its nests.

I am overwhelmed by deadly loss and burning longings.

So, you find me wandering in the streets alone, hardly forcing the steps of my life to move forward.

I keep accompanying my sad heart, consoling its continuous bleeding, and collecting the package of all the sins of my lifetime.

And so, I feel so tired, rather exhausted, after you distance your chest away from me.

13

O You! Poet!

You, O poet! Behold the crystal palaces, you built for yourself ,were all shattered and fallen down to small pieces.

As soon as you had come to inhabit them, they all collapsed on you, on the shelves of your books, smashing all your pens, and scattering your notebooks and papers everywhere.

This kept you away from the beautiful child inside you, made you long to fall into the arms of your mother, and quench your thirst.

As your mother is the source of tenderness, you can cry out your heart.

Sure, she is the only one who understands you, covers your tears, and hides your weakness.

She knows that you love to be a poet, you love to be a writer, and to be happy.

She is the only one who knows that you learned the first letters of the alphabet from her, and the first letters you uttered were the letters of her name.

So, she will not let the creative little poet die inside you.

She will never let your creative potentials fade away.

And so, you will never stop calling her "mama", a word that has a rhythmic and musical tone.

This woman who brought up you as a talented poet, well-versed writer, and strong lecturer.

You will neither speak, nor converse comprehendingly except with the poet.

You will not be able to give strength except to the poet's son.

So help me, O great mother! Give a new birth to this little child, restore to him his lost toys, his papers, his pens and his inkwell, give him a little space for romance and a dreamy life.

Give back to him his pink dreams, make him run after the rainbow, make him collect for us a bundle of daffodils and daisies.

Here are my pens and papers.

Pick out from them whatever you desire.

We are the ones who live for poetry, and not the vice versa.

We will restore to you your lost happiness and we will keep distance from the cities of sadness in which you dwell, only because we love you deeply: we love you more than ourselves.

Poetry is our journey together, O steadfast Pharaoh, O resident of the city of "Sinblaween", which I have never seen, nor been to.

However, I saw it in the sparkle of your sad eyes.

I also tasted literature and poetry in the meanings of your beautiful words, and its sweet tones.

Your withered looks reflect the beautiful Egyptian countryside with its splendor, serene nights, and purity.

Such little child within you will never die, nor will the poet, within you, ever leave you.

I finally decided to leave you alone, by yourself, so that you would feel bored, so that you would get sick and tired of your cold tough life, which was full of numbers and rough ,solid hands like iron.

I will leave you alone with a harsh, insignificant life.

So, you will long for my romance, for a warm and flowing life, which is adorned with beautiful words.

I will leave you alone with sparkling eyes, papers, books ,and poems composed by Nizar Qabbani[10].

You will long for freedom, for lying with your back on a green land.

You will miss playing with the stream water, walking on valleys, drinking cups of coffee, and sitting in the summer night breezes, under the grapevines, or the tall willow trees.

You will find in them the crystal palaces that contain you and will never be shattered.

Yes, they will contain you whether you are in full force or in your moments of weakness.

They will never betray you, as they are the storehouse of your secrets, and the secret of your strength.

They only can break the bars of sadness that surround you and provide you with pleasure.

Your loftiness is perceived greater than the pyramids, and your bounteous giving is more than the earth and rain when they meet.

The poet is always the only one who suffers, the only one who feels more than others.

He is a cloud of feelings and a planet of sincere feelings.

He shuns hypocrisy, cheating and manipulation, and all the things that have nothing to do with life and humanity.

The poet rejoices quickly and grieves quickly just like children.

I know that you love freedom more than life and ambition itself.

---

[10] **Nizar Qabbani was a Syrian diplomat, poet, writer and publisher.** [10]

I know that you always want to be like birds soaring high, landing on the ground, and also flying in the sky whenever they want.

You want no obstacle or barrier stop you from your goal.

You skip all the questions that are related to restricting your freedom, even if they are imaginary.

You want to be understood without saying anything.

You want someone to dive into your depths without asking for your permission, to search all times asking about you, but not to ask you about anything.

You want someone to understand your questions that you have never asked, and to answer them without asking your permission.

What would you do without coffee cups, books, pens and paper?

What would you do without this little child wreaking havoc inside you?

This little child who laughs to the point that laughter chokes him, and weeps to the point that salty tears wash his handsome face.

Here in my beautiful kindergarten I am waiting for you.

Here, with my papers, all the books and some pens I am waiting for your doodling.

I am extending my hand towards you. Will you drink a cup of coffee or tea with me?

I will wait until the little child returns within you. you will search for romance.

You will search for the beautiful autumn breeze.

You will search for the colors of spring and summer.

You will be attracted by the pose of my sitting in front of the sea.

I am sure that you will come to read me some of your poems, and to read me your latest publications.

You will come to me because you will definitely not let the little girl die of pain and sadness.

I know that you will come because you will not let this talent die inside me.

I am coming to you from the oldest province, from the oldest mountains in human history and geography.

I know that the child inside you will help me.

And in helping me you will live again; you will be the true man as it must be.

14

A message of love and apology

At this very time, I felt great pain, as I knew the story of your being late for the meeting.

I felt so sad that my depths were crumbled.

I was the only one to be responsible, as I always insisted on you, and wanted you in any way.

Indeed, love that generates selfishness suffocates and hurts its originator.

I have no wish to be that person who limits the greatness of a person.

On the contrary, I wish to be the cause, in some way or another, of supporting the one I love to ascend to the highest places of success and sophistication.

I wish him to be a distinguished person with his mind, his style, his way of thinking, and his way of living and enjoying it.

I owe you an apology a million times, for it is the last time I get angry with you for no reason other than your being busy with your work.

I promise you that this week I will start my intensive program for my academic exam, as well as my progressive course in the English language, which is a nice opportunity for me to prove myself worthy.

It is hard for me to stand before you while you are a great scholar.

Yet, my credit is empty of everything, except for a heart that beats for your love.

I must take advantage of you standing by my side and encouraging me to achieve what I have aspired to throughout my life.

For the sake of knowledge, I gave up many things, defied many circumstances, and I heard many hurtful words from the people of my town.

It was only my "father," may God have mercy on him, who understood this ambition and this strange love for study and development.

Your love alone is the greatest asset in my life to stand out as a shining star above all the planets of the whole sphere.

God Almighty bestowed upon me many things that He did not bestow on others, but, in return, I did not offer anything for myself and for these divine gifts.

However, now I have better conditions and very great capabilities: books, the internet, discs, and the freedom to travel anywhere to attend any seminar, conference, research, or the like.

It is true that my town is far away from other cities, but whoever wants can come, and I am self-taught and used to learn everything from research, books, and questioning.

Even when I took up my job in a judicial bailiff's office, I knew nothing about the law, for I had no academic study.

So, I noticed ridiculous looks in the eyes of the employees because they are university students and law students.

However, my boss made me in charge of all matters, to the extent that I would deputize for him in his absence in everything.

On the other hand, the employees used to tell me the wrong information whenever I asked them about something.

Nevertheless, in just four months I surpassed them all, and that was because I only used to read law books at night and on weekends.

I had much more time and even at break time, I was used to working, attending lessons from the first year at the university to the fourth and final year.

 After that, I photographed all the books and lessons of the professor at the university and read them all.

I brought various books from several places, until the judges themselves began to discuss several cases with me, and the lawyers and clients only spoke with me.

However, sometimes my professor got annoyed with me because they refused to talk to him in my absence.

I attended several conferences, to which my manager took me.

Likewise, the president of the chamber or the head of the councils and courts department invited me to them.

 All of this aroused more jealousy around me, and I was exposed to many abuses.

At that time, I knew that this job was far less than my ambitions and capabilities as well, and that it was just a stage, nothing less or more, so I went back to my previous plan and took my first steps in it.

But my illness, which took four years of my life and more, took away many things from me and I lost a lot because of it.

However, God Almighty compensated me with you, and with your being in my life. So, I love you more than anything else.

I regard the chance of my illness as something good for me because God has compensated me with a great light.

He has compensated me with a great source of knowledge and of life itself, so I must keep this light and drink from this source as much as I can.

Now, I am facing a great challenge, and I must win it, God willing. I have prepared my tools as before. Now I just have to work hard, stay up late, read and study.

First, I have to pass this exam, which is the only step that will prevent me from reaching anything.

It will take place in June, and the results will be in July.

I must also master English, develop more in Arabic, and study computers so that I know all the current sciences that are the revolution of this age.

You, for sure, are the leader of this.

Yet, you are absent from the Arab countries, including Algeria.

For this reason, I have collected some books, of which you will be the judge and my teacher as well.

After a year, I will come to your kingdom to be judged and hear your ruling.

The following is an example of God's mercy and kindness.

Among the so many stories I have heard and known, there was the story of a painter who developed his talent without entering an academic school or fine arts.

And how much he toiled even though his real job had nothing to do with art.

But, one year, when he decided to develop, he confined himself at home for a period of twelve months.

He only slept one hour because he believed in his abilities and potentials.

After that he greatly developed his art to the point that he became the painter of Queen Elizabeth of Britain and other international celebrities who would invite him to their palaces taking him in their private planes.

You can apply the same previous example to those who worked hard a great deal to learn other sciences and obtain other cultures.

According to me, failure is never the end, rather it has not diminished my resolution.

On the contrary, in every failure I learn new lessons. I just hate living in my country for only one thing, which is people's view of a divorced, unmarried woman.

They pour their looks of pity on her, because for them a woman must be married, and have a home and children.

But otherwise, she is viewed as a desperate woman.

Her success, whatever it is, will not compensate her for the family she establishes and the children she gives birth to.

It does not matter how she raises them.

Likewise, I hate the men's view of the divorced woman, as she becomes the coveted of everyone, and exposed to harassment by others.

They try to exploit her whenever she tries to claim her rights and achieve her ambition.

It is as if they give her something out of charity, and it is not her right.

So, they do not distinguish between what is permissible and what is forbidden.

This is what saddens me and makes me hate living in Algeria.

Even a woman's view of a divorced woman is negative.

However, I tried to prove to everyone that a divorced woman is just like others and that she is the one who imposes her respect on everyone and that she can achieve many things.

She is also able to live without a man and without sex, because she has goals greater than that.

She is a sublime, delicate and sensitive creature.

She deserves a man who loves her, marries her, protects her, develops her, and gives her the real value she deserves.

Without this condition there is no meaning to life and there should be no man in her life.

All my years since my divorce were very difficult and a great challenge.

Whenever I went to merry occasions or weddings, all the fingers would point to me as I was divorced, as if divorce was a great sin that I had committed.

Although no one was able to declare that to me directly because my response would not be expected, especially since I always look prettier and younger than all of them. I was the focus of everyone's attention.

All divorced women suffer from the same thing.

So, they are forced to marry anyone.

The important thing is that they get rid of the view of society and relatives on them.

They would prefer to live with any man, even if love had no existence in their lives or even began.

The couple became alienated after few years.

For this reason, I no longer go to any occasions, weddings or holidays.

Little by little, a very bitter loneliness was imposed on me.

Despite that I did not abandon my dream and my principles.

My family was the most beautiful thing in the world I had.

My dad, may God have mercy on him, was the greatest supporter in my life and he always pushed me to live the life I desire and not the life people desire, as living one's lives is a far reached goal for all people.

I'm sorry, every time you get a headache with the scribbles of my pain, but sometimes a person's suffering greatly limits his determination and burdens him.

Perhaps now I know the main reason why I hate living in Algeria because I never feel comfortable, and I know why I care about you in such a crazy way?

Because I am the only one who knows the value of love, I alone can value it more than any other human being, I have spent a long life searching for it.

My life was like someone walking on thorns, stones and embers.

I endured all that because I can only be in the bosom of a heart that loves me madly.

My father, may God have mercy on him, was my sociable person, and he was the one I talked to every morning and every evening.

He was the one I cheered for every day.

After his departure, I felt that I was stripped of everything.

I became lonely every evening, as if I was stripped of my strength, and of his cover and protection.

Only his words remained ringing inside my ears, his loud laughter and everything in him.

How much I miss my father every day.

How much my heart longs to meet him and talk to him, instead of staying for several days not talking to anyone.

He was alone accompanying me and we talked a lot and no one could understand the relationship between us because he was divulging all his pains and secrets with me.

Even when he wanted to complain about one of his children, he used to come to me because I used to contain him.

My father was a companion, brother, friend, and caring father.

I have never seen a man so tender in his own way nor as kind as him.